The **Essential** Buyer's Guide

PORSCHE

924

All models 1976 to 1988

T0373949

Your marque expert:
Steve Hodgkins

VELOCE PUBLISHING

THE PUBLISHER OF FINE AUTOMOTIVE BOOKS

www.veloce.co.uk

First published in November 2012 by Veloce Publishing Limited, Veloce House, Parkway Farm Business Park, Middle Farm Way, Poundbury, Dorchester, Dorset, DT1 3AR, England.
Fax 01305 250479/e-mail info@veloce.co.uk/web www.veloce.co.uk or www.velocebooks.com.

ISBN: 978-1-845844-09-7 UPC: 6-36847-04409-1

Readers with ideas for automotive books, or books on other transport or related hobby subjects, are invited to write to the editorial director of Veloce Publishing at the above address.
British Library Cataloguing in Publication Data – A catalogue record for this book is available from the British Library Typesetting, design and page make-up all by Veloce Publishing Ltd on Apple Mac. Printed in India by Replika Press.

Introduction
– the purpose of this book

Often overlooked, Porsche 924s provide a robust, exciting and practical solution for anyone seeking classic motoring on a budget.

For those new to the series, the 924 model was introduced in 1976. From relatively simple beginnings, the range spawned six models, and numerous special editions during its production run up to 1988, with its 2.0-litre engines (latterly 2.5-litre in the 924S) producing between 125bhp and a staggering 375bhp!

Whilst not a 911, the 924 series, in all of its guises, offers an inexpensive entry into the Porsche family.

A Series 1 924 Turbo.

This Buyer's Guide provides you with a comprehensive description of the various models, common faults, and what to look for and avoid when purchasing a 924 in any of its derivations.

Separate chapters are dedicated to making sure it's the right car for you, and reviewing the potential costs of ownership. Different models and their values are compared, together with likely problem areas, and how to inspect your potential purchase. Price guides in classic car magazines, such as *Classics Monthly* and *Practical Classics,* can often give a good idea of what to pay.

Chapter 9's easy-to-use buying calculator provides a method of working out a prospective purchase's overall condition, by adding up points relating to each area of the car being viewed. Some simple, common sense rules are offered to ensure you buy the best car available for your budget, and to allow you to enjoy many years of happy motoring as a Porsche owner.

924 Turbo wheel.

The relative merits of buying privately, at a garage, or through auctions (both on and offline) are considered, and documentation to be sought in a purchase is discussed, as well as restoration options.

Lastly, there's an informative section detailing chassis and engine numbers.

Porsche is the registered trademark of Dr Ing hc F Porsche AG. The publisher of this book is not affiliated or associated in any way with Porsche AG, Porsche Cars Great Britain Limited, Porsche Cars of North America Inc, or any other Porsche Group subsidiary.

Foreword and thanks

Having owned a number of 924s, 924 Turbos, and latterly a 924 Carrera GT, over the last 20 years, it's fair to say that I'm a great fan of this often overlooked model. I still get great pleasure from looking after and driving a 'junior' supercar and hope that this book will help you decide to join the 924 family and enable you to buy a good example of the marque.

A large number of people have helped in collating information and photographs for this book. In particular, my thanks go to Steve Cooper of the 924 Owners' club, Jon Mitchell and Mark Kemp of JMG in Christchurch Dorset, Scott McNulty of OPC Bournemouth, Paul Hedges, 924 Register Secretary of the Porsche Club GB, Graham Pearson, Richard Kirk, Gmund Cars, Trefor and Claire Willingham, and Porsche AG. The vital stats and model information was collated from Peter Morgan's excellent title *The Porsche 924/944 Book*, ISBN 1859608647.

The front cover, CGT interior (chapter 4), Fuchs wheel (chapter 7), and open sunroof shots (chapter 9) are courtesy of Steve Bennett, Editor of *911 and Porsche World*.

A gathering of Carrera GTs.

The Essential Buyer's Guide™ currency

At the time of publication a BG unit of currency "⬤" equals approximately £1.00/US$1.59/Euro 1.26. Please adjust to suit current exchange rates using Sterling as the base unit.

Contents

1 Is it the right car for you?
– marriage guidance

As a classic purchase for everyday or weekend use, the 924 is still noted by owners for its comfort, looks, and ability to carry two adults and two (smallish) children in comfort, plus two sets of golf clubs (hidden from prying eyes by a roller blind), whilst still returning 30mpg. With rear seats folded, 924s can carry a considerable amount of luggage.

Controls
The 924 was designed in the 1970s and, as such, most models have no power steering, making for hard work manoeuvring at slow speeds. The brakes and clutch are nicely weighted, however the steering column has no adjustment, which can prove uncomfortable for taller people.

Turbos have a 'dogleg' gear lever: first gear is across and back, with reverse across and forward (where normal gearboxes locate first gear).

Will it fit in your garage?
Length: 13ft 8in (4216mm)
Width: 5ft 5in (1687mm)
Height: 4ft 2in (1270mm)

Usability
The standard 924 easily keeps up with modern traffic, and can exceed the speed limit when circumstances permit. Large, lift-out sunroofs provide glorious summer motoring, and a few cars have optional air-conditioning. Galvanised bodies on all but the earliest cars means rust issues are less common than would be experienced with other marques of this age.

Parts availability
Other than some trim, most spare parts are easy to find. Inexpensive, secondhand parts regularly appear on internet auction sites.

924 boot (trunk) with rear seats up ...

... and with rear seats down, showing the large carrying capacity.

The Turbo's 'dogleg' gearlever.

924 with updated wheels.

Insurance
The cars are classed in Group 17 or 18, although cheaper insurance can often be obtained through classic car insurance schemes.

Running costs
Generally reasonable – detailed in chapter 2.

Prices and investment potential
924s can be purchased from a few hundred pounds up to several thousand pounds for a concours example. Prices have been stable for some time, but are now starting to rise as good condition cars become harder to find.

Alternatives
MGB GT, Jensen Healey estate, Reliant Scimitar, Volvo P1800S, Datsun 240Z, Ford Capri, and Triumph GT6.

A trio of green Turbos.

The 924 Turbo's NACA air duct.

2 Cost considerations
- affordable, or a money pit?

Joining at least one of the major Porsche clubs has many benefits, including technical advice, access to other owners, and, in many cases, discounts on parts and labour at nominated dealers throughout the country.

Servicing intervals
924 Porsches need an interim service every 6000 miles (10,000 km) or six months, and an annual service every 12,000 miles (20,000 km) or 12 months. Major services are required every two years and include brake and clutch fluid changes. Cambelt (timing belt) changes are required at 48,000 miles (80,000km) or every four years. 924S models should ideally have their balance and timing belts, front engine oil seals, and waterpumps changed at 80,000 miles (125,000km) or at eight year intervals. Automatic 'boxes should have a gearbox service (oil, gasket and filter) every 80,000 miles (125,000km) or eight years.

Servicing costs
These indicative costs show the likely average cost from independent Porsche specialists. Official Porsche Centres are still happy to work on the 924 range, and sometimes offer discounted rates. (Prices correct at the time of publication.)

Interim service: ●x140
Annual major service: ●x250
Manual: ●x17 (*Porsche 924 and Turbo 1976-1985 Owner's workshop manual* by JH Haynes and Charles Lipton, 924S not covered)
Official workshop manuals (924 inc Turbo): ●x295 (www.gmundcollection.com) or ●x347 (Porsche) (assumes existing engineering experience)

Additional service items costs (inc labour) (924/Turbo/S)
Cambelt (timing belt) replacement: ●x120/175/250
Brake and clutch fluid changes: ●x60
Front brake discs & pads: ●x200/245/300:
Rear brake drums/discs & pads: ●x286/265/265
Clutch replacement: ●x585/850/660
Turbo replacement: ●x1400
Wheel alignment (full geometry check): ●x115

Mechanical parts (924/Turbo/S)
These are indicative costs; actual costs will vary slightly depending on model.
Oil filter: ●x6
Fuel filter: ●x26
Air filter: ●x18
Full exhaust system: ●x420
Brake master cylinder: ●x140
Clutch master/slave cylinder: ●x73/49
Radiator (exchange): ●x207
Alternator (exchange): ●x122

Starter motor (exchange): ●x132
Water pump: ●x42
Wheel bearing kit: ●x20
Shock absorbers, front (each): Insert ●x49; Leg ●x166
Shock absorbers, Rear (each): ●x64
Springs (pair): ●x104
Trackrod end: ●x19
Rebuilt engine: ●x3000/4000/5000
Rebuilt gearbox: ●x2000
Steering rack (exchange): ●x154
Fuel pump: ●x136

Body parts/paintwork
Windscreen: ●x250
Rear glass screen: ●x 50 (secondhand)
Front wing (new Porsche): ●x640
Headlight: ●x30
Door (new Porsche): ●x1250 (●x50 secondhand)
Full respray (inc preparation): ●x3000-5000
Wheel refurbishment: ●x75
New tyre: ●x75

Interior retrim
Full front seat retrim (each): ●x525
Carpet replacement: N/A new. ●x50 secondhand.
Headlining: ●x298

Used parts
Porsche breakers can assist (see advertisements in Club magazines as well as classic car magazines). Internet auction sites also have a good range of used parts. Specialist Porsche trimmers can often help with hard to find trim items.

3 Living with a 924
– will you get along together?

Delightfully, the Porsche 924, 924 Turbo, and 924S are inexpensive to buy, can be run on a budget, and still give thrills and excitement which far outweigh the money spent.

Remarkably, after some 30 years, Porsche 924s still rank as one of the most practical sports cars for daily driving. Comfortable, with excellent all-round vision (aided by the large wrap-around rear screen), the car can easily keep up with modern day traffic. Whether used as a weekend fun car, or for the daily school run, a good example that's well maintained will give years of trouble-free service for a fraction of the cost of a new sports coupé.

Good points
• A fully galvanised body (from model year 1980) means less corrosion than similar cars of the '70s and '80s.
• Simple four-cylinder engines without complicated electronic control units (ECUs) means they're simple to look after (especially for the DIY enthusiast).
• Workshop manuals are readily available.
• Transaxle gearbox (at the rear of the car) gives almost 50:50 weight distribution, providing excellent, safe, controllable handling and good grip.
• Light, spacious interior provides generous 2+2 seating.
• Opening rear hatch provides access to large boot (trunk) with privacy blind to hide luggage from view.

Plenty of room for suitcases.

Comfortable 924 interior.

Luggage, hidden from view.

924 adapted for track use.

• Excellent fuel consumption for a sporty car (around 30mpg).
• In general, spare parts are inexpensive.
• Comfortable seats.
• Nicely weighted controls.
• Easy to drive in town, yet a great Grand Tourer.
• Inexpensive to purchase a really good example.
• Little or no depreciation.
• Turbos offer spectacular performance when on boost. 924S can readily be adapted for track days.
• 924S has the later 944's engine, offering more torque and performance than the heavier 944 which followed.
• Some three-speed automatics were made for a more relaxed driving experience.
• A thriving club scene with all regions of the country represented, offering advice, meetings and a chance to become a member of the Porsche family.

Bad points
• Lack of power steering on most models makes low speed parking hard work.
• Trim now hard to find (although specialist trimmers – see chapter 16 – can recreate most pieces at a cost).
• Rear seats are really only suitable for small children.
• Values mean restorations are not financially viable.
• Replacing turbos can incur large labour costs.
• Cars can be prone to electrical faults.
• Few cars have air-conditioning fitted.

4 Relative values
– which model for you?

Whilst there were three mainstream models of 924 (924, Turbo, and S) throughout the model's life, there were many special editions and racing derivations. Below is a list of the main models produced and their value relative to each other, expressed as a percentage. Differences between models is detailed in chapter 17.

924 (1976–85)
1984cc four-speed, and later five-speed manual and three-speed automatic, 125bhp.
40%

924 Lux Coupé.

924 Le Mans special edition.

924 Turbo (Mk1 1978–81/Mk2 1981–83)
1984cc five-speed (dogleg first gear) manual 170/177bhp.
50%/55%

924 Turbo ...

... and inside, with optional leather trim.

924 Carrera GT (1981)
1984cc five-speed (dogleg first gear) manual 210bhp.
85%

A pair of 924 Carrera GTs.

924 Carrera GT inside.

924 Carrera GTS (1981)

1984cc five-speed (dogleg first gear) 245bhp (or 280bhp Club Sport specification).
100%

924 S (1986–88)

2500cc five-speed manual and three-speed automatic 150bhp.
55%

A number of special edition 924s were produced throughout the model's life to celebrate racing victories or to boost sales in different countries. Relative values depend on condition and originality – perhaps up to five per cent more than the mainstream cars above.

924 Carrera GTR

As only 19 of this extremely rare and specialised model were believed to have been produced, this particular variant isn't pertinent to this book.

924 Carrera GT and GTS together.

924S Le Mans special edition, front and rear.

5 Before you view
– be well informed

To avoid a wasted journey and the disappointment of finding that a car does not match your expectations, it will help if you're very clear about what questions you want to ask or think about before you pick up the telephone. Some of these points might appear basic, but when you're excited about the prospect of buying your dream classic, it's amazing how some of the most obvious things slip your mind. Also, check the current values of the models in which you are interested, in classic car magazines which give both a price guide and auction results.

Where is the car?
Is it going to be worth travelling hundreds of miles to the next county/state? A locally advertised car, although it may not sound very interesting, can add to your knowledge for very little effort, so make a visit – it might even be in better condition than expected. If bidding on an internet auction site, bear in mind how far you will have to travel to collect the car or the cost of delivery.

Dealer or private sale
Establish early on if the car is being sold by its owner or by a trader. A private owner should have all the history, so don't be afraid to ask detailed questions. A dealer may have more limited knowledge of a car's history, but should have some documentation. A dealer may offer a warranty/guarantee (ask for a printed copy and check what is covered and the amount of each claim) and finance.

Cost of collection and delivery
A dealer may well be used to quoting for delivery by car transporter. A private owner may agree to meet you halfway, but only agree to this after you have seen the car at the vendor's address to validate the documents. Conversely, you could meet halfway and agree the sale, but insist on meeting at the vendor's address for the handover.

When and where to view?
It is always preferable to view at the vendor's home or business premises. In the case of a private sale, the car's documentation should tally with the vendor's name and address. Arrange to view only in daylight and avoid a wet day. Most cars look better in poor light or when wet.

Reason for sale?
Do make this one of the first questions. Why is the car being sold and how long has it been with the current owner? How many previous owners are shown? Consider contacting the previous owner to verify the details being given if in doubt.

Left- to right-hand drive/specials and convertibles
If a steering conversion has been done it can only reduce the value and it may well be that other aspects of the car still reflect the specification for a foreign market.
 Some of the more racing orientated 924 models are only available in left-hand drive format, so carrying out some research before viewing is essential when

considering purchasing one of these models. Contacting a club specialist for more information is always worthwhile.

Condition (body/chassis/interior/mechanicals)
Ask the seller for an honest appraisal of the car's condition. Ask specifically about some of the check items described in chapter 7.

All original specification
An original equipment car is invariably of higher value than a customised version.

If changes have been made, ask if the original equipment is available as part of the purchase.

Matching data/legal ownership
Check that the VIN/chassis, engine numbers, and licence plate match the official registration document. Is the owner's name and correct address recorded in the official registration documents?

Ask who the car is insured with – seeing the owner's insurance certificate also helps confirm ownership, and the company may offer good deals for this type of car.

For those countries that require an annual test of roadworthiness, does the car have a document showing it complies. This is the MoT certificate in the UK, which can be verified on 0300 123 9000 or at www.direct.gov.uk/checkyourmot.

If required, does the car carry a current road fund licence/licence plate tag?

Does the vendor own the car outright? Several organisations will supply the data on ownership, based on the car's licence plate number, for a fee. The information should advise if your proposed purchase is stolen, recorded as having been in an accident, has outstanding finance, or is being sought by the Police or an Insurance company. In the UK, the following organisations can supply vehicle ownership data:

HPI   0845 300 8905 www.hpicheck.com
AA   0800 316 3564 www.theaa.com/car-data-checks
DVLA (Vehicle Identity Check)   0300 123 9000 www.direct.gov.uk
RAC   0800 975 5867 www.rac.co.uk
Experian   www.autocheck.co.uk

Other countries will have similar organisations.

Unleaded fuel
All 924s can run on unleaded fuel.

Insurance
Check with your existing insurer before setting out. It's worth obtaining an insurance quote to ensure you are comfortable with the likely premium before buying the car and your current policy might not cover you to drive the car if you do purchase it.

How you can pay
Check with the seller what is an acceptable method of payment. A cheque/check will take several days to clear and the seller may prefer to sell to a cash buyer.

However, a banker's draft (a cheque issued by a bank) is as good as cash, but safer, so contact your own bank and become familiar with the formalities that are necessary to obtain one. If nervous of carrying large amounts of cash, agree to carry out the financial transaction at a branch of your bank if you decide to buy the car.

Alternatively, if you trust the seller, an online bank transfer avoids having to handle cash.

Buying at auction?
If the intention is to buy at auction, see chapter 10 for further advice.

Professional vehicle check (mechanical examination)
There are often marque/model specialists who will undertake professional examination of a vehicle on your behalf, and it is worth contacting them before you view the vehicle. Owners' clubs will be able to put you in touch with such specialists. A genuine seller should have no reservations about such an examination.

Alternatively, in the UK, official Porsche Centres will carry out a 111-point check for a potential 924 purchase for around £140 +VAT.

Other organisations that will carry out a general professional check in the UK are:

AA   0800 056 8040 (motoring organisation with vehicle inspectors)
RAC   0800 085 2529 (motoring organisation with vehicle inspectors)

Other countries will have similar organisations.

6 Inspection equipment
– these items will really help

Before you rush out of the door, gather together a few items that will help as you work your way around the car.

This book
This book is designed to be your guide at every step, so take it along and use the check boxes in chapter 9 to help you assess each area of the car you're interested in. Don't be afraid to let the seller see you using it.

Reading glasses (if you need them for close work)
Take your reading glasses if you need them to read documents and make close up inspections.

Magnet (not powerful, a fridge magnet is ideal)
A magnet will help you check if the car is full of filler, or has fibreglass panels. Ask the seller's permission before using a magnet, and if permission is granted, use the magnet to sample bodywork areas all around the car, but be careful not to damage the paintwork. Expect to find a little filler here and there, but not whole panels. There's nothing wrong with fibreglass panels, but a purist might want the car to be as original as possible. Also bear in mind some models were meant to have fibreglass wings!

Torch (flashlight)
A torch with fresh batteries will be useful for peering into the wheel arches and under the car.

Probe (a small screwdriver works very well)
A small screwdriver can be used – with care – as a probe, particularly in the wheelarches and on the underside and sills. With this you should be able to check an area of severe corrosion, but be careful – if it's really bad the screwdriver might go right through the metal!

Overalls
Be prepared to get dirty. Take along a pair of overalls, if you have them, and something dry to lie on when looking underneath the body. A chamois leather to dry the car if it's wet is also handy.

Mirror on a stick
Fixing a mirror at an angle on the end of a stick may seem odd, but you'll probably need it to check the condition of the underside of the car. It will also help you to peer into some of the important crevices and look for oil leaks around the engine bay. You can also use it, together with the torch, along the underside of the sills and on the floor.

Digital camera
If you have the use of a digital camera, take it along so that later you can study

some areas of the car more closely. Take a picture of any part of the car that causes you concern, and seek a friend's opinion (or ask a specialist from one of the clubs).

A friend, preferably a knowledgeable enthusiast

Ideally, have a friend or knowledgeable enthusiast accompany you – a second opinion without 'rose tinted specs' is always valuable.

Exterior

Start by walking around the car. Does it sit properly? Too low means tired or non-standard suspension. Look along each side: are there ripples or 'supermarket dings' in the bodywork? Check the panel gaps; are they even? How is the paintwork: is it shiny or dull? Red paint in particular goes 'flat' and 'milky' over the years if not looked after (see chapter 14). Check each panel for rust; there should be very little, as these cars were partly or fully galvanised, depending on when they were built. The valance and the front of the bonnet is likely to have a few stone chips, but this is quite normal for a car of this age.

Seen better days.

Use a weak magnet to check for filler in the panels. If present, satisfy yourself as to why.

Is the glass chipped/cracked or delaminating at the edges? Are there any identifying marks on the glass (etched security numbers, for example), and do they match? Is the make of the glass the same (other than perhaps for the front windscreen, which may have been replaced).

Check the wheels; are they kerbed, chipped, and in need of refurbishment, or are they in good condition? Refurbishing wheels costs approximately ●x75 per wheel, so factor this into your price negotiation.

Look through the wheels to the discs; are they scored, with a lip around the outside edge (worn), or rusty (showing the car is little used)? Does the car have matched tyres, and how much tread is left on them?

Lift the bonnet and check the wing bolts; do they look original or has the car had new wings? Again, obtain a satisfactory answer or walk away.

In need of refurbishment.

Check the wheelarches: some chips and damage will be inevitable, but is the damage commensurate with the mileage and history of the car? Visually check the condition of the exhaust.

Check all the seals around the doors, rear glass screen, and sunroof, if fitted. Are they damaged or hard? If so, can water pass through? Lifting the carpets and checking the floor can reveal if leaks are present.

Check that the doors haven't dropped by watching them as they close; do they lift into their catches, or close easily.

Sills can rust, so check under any plastic sill protectors, and prod the underneath with a screwdriver to see if the metal is solid. Check around aerial holes to make sure rust isn't present.

Check the badging: a Porsche crest should be

Model identification decal.

fitted to the front panel, and a decal on the rear right-hand side of the boot (trunk) panel in Porsche script, detailing the model.

Engine bay
Check the suspension turrets and crossmembers under the engine, for signs of accident damage. Look at the condition of the engine oil as an indicator of when the car was last serviced (and compare with the seller's answer). Also, check the general state of the engine bay: are the wiring terminals corroded, is everything 'dusty' (good) or 'oily' (not so good)? Are the rubber belts in good condition or in need of changing? Ask when the cambelt was last changed.

Interior
Start with the carpets; are they worn or faded? With the owner's permission, lift the floor mats to check for holes, particularly the driver's footwell area, and, if possible, lift the carpets to check the footwell floor condition. Severe rust or holes should not be present.

Lift the rear carpet and check the condition of the spare wheel well at the back of the car, as well as the storage compartments each side of the spare wheel. Whilst there, check if the spare wheel is in good condition, and, if it's a 'run flat' space saving wheel, is the compressor and full toolkit available with the

Spacesaver spare wheel.

car? Check for accident damage, too, and, ideally, the presence of a self-adhesive paper sticker on the inside of the rear panel (although after 30 years, this may well have been removed).

Next, check the condition of the seats. Whilst the rear seats are usually in good condition, the driver's front seat fabric can split from the leatherette along the seams. Similarly, the

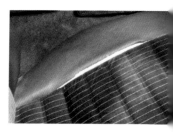
Split in the driver's seat.

Sticker on rear panel of boot (trunk).

driver's bolster can wear due to the constant rubbing it gets from the driver getting in and out of the car.
Leather upholstery, if fitted, should be inspected for condition and wear in the same way.

Check that all the buttons and dials work, especially the front headlight washers if fitted, the rear screen wiper and the electric windows, all of which can suffer from electrical problems. Check the wear of the pedal rubbers against the stated mileage.

If fitted, is the air-conditioning very cold? Is the steering wheel in good condition (either three-spoke or four-spoke)? Gear knobs are made from fine leather and usually wear quite badly (although they can be recovered by specialist trimmers).

Lastly, check the dash for cracks. Nearly all dashboards will have cracks of one form or another, due to the differential expansion of the materials from which they are made. Use this as a negotiating point.

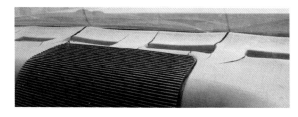

Extreme cracking on the dashboard.

Mechanicals

Ask the seller to start the car from cold: 924s sometimes have cold starting problems, and, indeed, some have hot starting problems, but specialists have the knowledge to cure these issues. The car should start easily. Check that no coloured smoke comes from the exhaust (if you decided to examine the car in greater depth, see chapter 9's Test drive section for more details on smoke issues).

On RHD cars, the handbrake is on the right of the driver's seat; check it holds the car on an incline. Check that the oil pressure at start-up is five to six bar, and at least two to three bar when running (be wary if the pressure falls below one bar). The voltmeter should charge at just under 14 volts.

Push down on each wing and at the rear corners of the car. The suspension should cause the car to bounce approximately one-and-a-half times. Any more than this, and the suspension is probably tired and may need replacing.

How to spot a fake 924 Carrera GT/GTS

Due to their value and scarcity, some replica 924 Carrera GT/GTSs have been created from 924 Turbos. Check the details below to ensure you purchase an original vehicle.

For the Carrera GT

Things to check: are the wings made of a flexible polyurethane/fibreglass mix? They should flex on the GT but not on the GTS. Is the indicator on the front wings long and thin rather than square? Does the engine (number starting with 3150) have the correct Langerer & Reich intercooler? Is the windscreen fitted with an incorrect rubber seal? Is

Carrera GTs.

the rear bumper longer than that of a 924 Turbo? The rear spoiler should be larger and rougher than a 924 Turbo. Are the correct Fuchs alloys fitted (7x15in or 16in front; 8x15in or 16in rear)? Does the interior have the correct 911 Sport seats, with brown/orange stripe fabric and orange piping? The right wing should have a large Carrera decal, and a smaller yellow 924 Carrera GT decal should be stuck to the

RHS engine bay inner wing. A large unique air scoop should be fitted to the bonnet, and brake cooling ducts should be fitted behind the front valance. It is worth checking the VIN (which for a CGT should be WPOZZZ93ZBN700 XXX, the last three characters being the serial number of the car, between 051 to 450) and checking with the Register secretary for the history of the car (most cars of this model are known to the club).

Classic Fuchs wheel.

For the Carrera GTS

As each of these 59 cars is likely to be slightly different (and extremely expensive), check with the PCGB Register secretary, and look for an extremely extensive history/provenance before considering purchase. VIN numbers for the cars are WPOZZZ93ZBS700 XX, the last characters being the serial number of the car between 01 and 59.

Carrera GTS.

Ownership/title/ paperwork

Time to check the paperwork. By now you will have built up a picture of the car – condition, mileage, how well looked after it is – and you are looking to confirm this view with the paperwork.

If you are looking for a restoration project (see chapter 13), you may be less concerned about condition and should focus on ownership, ie, is the car the owner's to sell and will you get a clear and valid title if you buy it? Price will be based upon condition and rarity. It's more likely that you're buying a car as a runner, and therefore condition is hugely important, as well as title.

So, first check the mileage of the car. Can it be confirmed by past MoT certificates and a full service history? Be a little cautious of stamps in the service history book without any supporting paperwork; unscrupulous car salesman have

22

been known to stamp a service book to increase the value of a car. Consider calling the garages in the service book, and asking them to check their computer records to verify that the service work has been done at the mileages shown. This goes a long way to evidencing a genuine car.

Is the overall condition commensurate with the mileage? Pedal rubbers, for example, don't wear out on genuine low mileage cars.

Is there a large sheath of bills? Again, this shows money has been spent on the car. Have any large repairs been carried out (money you won't have to spend)? Check especially when the cambelt was last changed on the 924 Turbo and S models (see the receipt), as this will be a very expensive repair should it break. If you buy the car and are uncertain when the cambelt was last changed, have it done straight away.

Look for specific model identifiers, stickers on the rear boot (trunk) panel of 924s, for example, or the yellow model identifier on the RHS of the engine bay inner wing.

Check the chassis Vehicle Identification Number (VIN), embossed into the front bulkhead in the engine bay on 924 model cars, or on the suspension turrets of very early cars. Does it match both the model range and the V5 (logbook)?

Check the engine serial number (on LHS of the crankcase next to the clutch) against the V5; does it match?

If buying a LHD car in a RHD country (or vice versa), check the correct import documents are present, and contact the importer if in doubt.

Finally, make sure the car is the purported owner's to sell. Does the address where you are viewing the car tie up with the address on the V5? Seeing the seller's address on their insurance certificate is an additional check for peace of mind.

Get a vehicle data check (details in chapter 5) to check the car is free from finance and has not had any accidents or been written-off.

For additional peace of mind, consider getting an OPC 111 point check, or get a specialist independent garage to check the car for you. This should include a cold start, so they will probably need the car overnight.

Walk away or stay?

Now you should know if further investigation is warranted; if so, chapter 9 covers all these areas in greater detail. Do bear in mind that many of these cars are now approaching 30 years old and really good ones are hard to find. However, good cars can be improved easily at minimal cost, and can provide exciting and cost efficient weekend fun cars or even daily drivers, so it's worth spending some time finding the right car for you.

If the car doesn't feel right, it probably isn't, so take your time to find the right one and don't be afraid to walk away. Other than the rare Carreras, there are generally plenty of examples for you to view. Whilst restoration may not be financially viable for most of the 924 models, it's covered more fully in chapter 13.

8 Key points
– where to look for problems

Check the condition of the body, paintwork, and the wheels: this car's paintwork is poor.

Check the general condition of the engine bay, and look for any large leaks or signs of accident damage. This car has definitely been standing for a while! The cambelt cover is missing, and rust is evident in the body on the left-hand side.

Regrettably, carpets fade with age. Wet/ damp could be indicative of a leak.

The driver's seat, particularly, splits along the seams.

Dashes crack – often quite severely.

Check the Vehicle Identification Number (VIN) against the registration document.

24

9 Serious evaluation
– 60 minutes for years of enjoyment

Score each section using the boxes as follows:
4 = excellent; 3 = good; 2 = average; 1 = poor. The totting up procedure is
detailed at the end of the chapter. Be realistic in your marking!

Exterior bodywork and panels

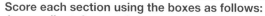

The main shell of the car was galvanised (the lower part from 1976, fully from 1980), which reduces the incidence of rust, although it won't eliminate it from a car that hasn't been cared for. Typically, rust starts at the lower edges of panels, or holes in the bodywork made for other reasons (eg, for the radio aerial) and develops unseen, often under rubber trim (as sometimes fitted to the sills) until it's too late and major

An extremely rusty sill.

remedial work is required. Gently prod suspect metal with a screwdriver to check for corrosion.

Check lower front valance condition.

Check each panel in turn, perhaps by rubbing your hand over it. Look for scratches, 'dings,' or irregularities in the paint finish. Check particularly the edges of the wheelarches and the wheelarches themselves, paying attention to the hidden recesses where mud builds-up and retains moisture, leading to rust. They will have been bombarded with road debris for 25 years or more, so some damage is to be expected. Check with a torch to see if holes have appeared, or if the damage is purely superficial. Look at the lower front valance for damage, and for rust in the seams where the valance meets the wings. Check also that the gutters on the roof of the car aren't rusting (particularly on early cars).

Stand back and check the shut lines around the bonnet and the doors. Are they even and do the panels sit flush against each other? Do the doors open and close easily without lifting or dropping? Make sure the door handles work properly and aren't seized.

Check the door hinges; are the screw heads still body coloured, or has a screwdriver scratched the screw heads, evidencing adjustment or removal and replacement of the doors? Look at the bottom of the doors; are they rusty, just dirty or, on cars that have been well looked after, clean? Check that the drain holes aren't blocked, which would cause water to lie at the bottom of the doors and lead to rust.

Check if the door hinge screws are unmarked.

Check the single jacking point on each side of the car (on the floorpan, roughly level with the middle of each sill). Is it intact and capable of supporting the car on a jack?

Check that the bonnet opens and closes easily and isn't out of alignment, which might mean the bonnet has been taken off. Similarly, check that the glass

Rust around rear hatch
pin recesses.

rear hatch opens and closes easily and sits squarely on the bodywork when shut. Check around the hatch pin recesses, as rust is often present here. If gas struts are fitted to either the bonnet or rear hatch, do they operate correctly, and actually support the bonnet and rear hatch when fully open? Struts wear and can occasionally fail.

Look at the door jambs for evidence of paint overspray, and check the condition of all the rubber seals around the doors, sunroof, and rear hatch. Are they perished, damaged or permanently compressed, which could allow water in? Do they spring back when pressed and still look fresh?

Check under the bonnet for signs of accident damage. Look at the chassis members at the bottom of the engine bay for signs of damage (creasing, welding, or a different paint finish), and also check the strut mounts and inner wings for any sign of damage.

Vehicle Identification Number (VIN)   ☑ ☑ ☑ ☑

Every vehicle produced should have a unique VIN. Be very wary if it doesn't match the paperwork. Early cars have a ten digit code, starting with the year of manufacture. For the 1981 year, Porsche changed its codes to 17 digits. (See chapter 17.)

Check the VIN.

Paint   ☑ ☑ ☑ ☑

See chapter 14 for likely paint problems. The paint code and German name of the colour are printed on a self-adhesive decal stuck to the bodywork behind the engine firewall, and (if still present) on the sticker attached to the rear panel of the car behind the carpet.

Check each panel is the same colour, and ask the seller if any panels have been repainted. On all but very original cars, expect some paintwork to have been resprayed: you're interested in how well it has been done, and how it matches the rest of the car. Look for raised straight lines of paint at the edge of panels (where masking tape has been removed), and pull back all the rubbers looking for evidence of masking tape lines or paint colour differences. Check also for overspray on wheels, wheelarches, and door jambs.

Exterior trim   ☑ ☑ ☑ ☑

Where fitted, check underneath any plastic sill protectors for corrosion. All 924s have a Porsche crest badge fitted to the front panel of the car. If faded, this is replaceable at minimal cost. 924 Turbos have rubber spoilers attached to the rear glass hatch (many standard 924s have also been retro-fitted with spoilers, as they improve the appearance of the car). These can perish with age, becoming pitted and discoloured.

924 Turbos also have black rubber bodywork protectors fitted at the back of the rear wheelarch.

Sill protectors on 924
Turbo.

924 Turbo rear spoiler.

924 Turbo spats.

Main production 924s have a decal denoting the model on the right-hand side of the rear bodywork, and Turbo models have the word 'turbo' on the inside sills, visible when the doors are open. Early 924s have a 'toothed' fuel filler cap, replaced by a standard cap under a flap in 1980.

Rear model decal.

Turbo decal on sills.

Early 'toothed' filler cap.

Wipers

Check the wipers' speeds (intermediate, normal speed, and fast), and that they sit properly at rest. Check that the driver's side wiper hasn't caught the edge of the bonnet and removed any paint. Note that the area of windscreen cleaned by the wipers is maximised for an LHD car.

Check that the rear wiper works when the switch is pressed (there can sometimes be electrical issues), and the condition of the motor box. If rattles are heard in a car, it can often be the rear wiper motor box that's to blame.

Rear wiper motor box.

Lights

Apart from the rare racing-derived GTS and GTR, all 924s have headlamps that pop up. This makes for an attractive aerodynamic profile when down, and the opposite when up – although it is usually dark, so not seen! Check the headlamps raise and lower easily and work when the headlamp switch below the dashboard dials is pressed to its second position; headlamp lifting motors can fail. Whilst the headlights are on, check the operation of the headlight washer jets by pressing the switch on the centre console. There is a second motor at the bottom of the large windscreen washer bottle, in the engine bay, that powers this feature and electrical gremlins are often present.

Centre console switches.

The foglamps work from one of the four switches on the console. Rear lamp clusters often crack; this can be an MoT failure if the crack allows white light through. Check that all of the front and back lights work correctly. Look for moisture in the lenses, which could indicate a failed seal, or movement of the unit, which requires the mounting brackets to be checked for corrosion or accident damage.

Glass ⁴ ③ ② ①

Check all the glass in the car for cracks or damage, together with the condition of the front screen rubber seal. Check the make of the glass, which should be the same around the car, apart, perhaps, from the front screen which may have been changed due to stone chip damage. Be cautious if different makes are seen, as replacement could be as a result of an accident.

The edge of the front screen can show delamination. Whilst replacement is relatively cheap (in the UK, prices start around ●x250 depending on your area), the rear screen is now unavailable. Buying a spare off an internet auction site may turn out to be a very cost effective investment for the future.

If it's a cold day and the glass is misted up, check the operation of the heated rear element.

Front screen: the 'milky' look is delamination.

Wheels ④ ③ ② ①

Standard 924s had four-stud 14in wheels, increasing to five-stud 15in wheels with the introduction of the 924 Turbo. Optional 16in wheels were available for the Turbo and Carrera GTs. See chapter 17 for tyre sizes.

Alloy wheel corrosion.

Check that the wheel centre caps are present.

Check all four wheels and the spare for condition and kerbing. Check particularly for alloy wheels showing milky-white corrosion, evidencing moisture creeping under the lacquer. Refurbishment costs a few hundred pounds, and this needs to be factored into the price as appropriate. Check that the wheel centre caps are present, as well as the relevant key if locking wheel nuts are fitted.

Tyres ④ ③ ② ①

Check the tyre's manufacturer and rating, looking, ideally, for a matched set of tyres on all four wheels –

or at least the front and rear pairs being the same make. A tyre's rating is denoted by a letter or letters next to the tyre size on the sidewall. An H rating covers cars that will do up to 130mph/210kph. A V rating covers cars that will do up to 149mph/240kph. Cars that can exceed this speed (924 Turbos and Carreras) require a Z, W, or Y rating. Other letters aren't appropriate. Tyre makes that have been approved by Porsche are given an N rating; this is totally independent of the tyres speed rating. If in doubt, check with a tyre fitting professional before buying new tyres for your car.

Check for uneven tyre wear (evidencing alignment issues), cracks or damage, and also the age of the tyre. It's generally recommended that tyres should be replaced if older than ten years. Also check the tread to see that the tyre is wearing evenly (to confirm the suspension is setup correctly) and how much tread is left. Whilst the legal limit in the UK is currently 1.6mm across 75 per cent of the tyre, the 924 is a high-powered sports car and 3mm is often considered to be a safer minimum, especially when driving in wet or winter conditions.

Cabin   4 3 2 1
First impressions are important and you should mark the overall condition before looking at specific items within the interior of the car.

Other than trim changes, the 924 interior remained constant throughout the model's life, and indeed for the early 944 models (useful when searching for parts).

The dashboard integrates nicely into the top of the door panels, and below it, on RHD cars, on the side panel of the passenger footwell, is the bonnet release handle. The main fusebox is located underneath the glovebox, with a secondary fusebox above.

Seats   4 3 2 1
The high backed seat design in 924s is very comfortable. The seats usually have leatherette backs and bolsters with a fabric insert. They are manually adjusted for front/rear movement (a bar at front, under the seat) and the backs can be released by a lever on the side of the seat to allow access to the rear seats. Some special editions are entirely fabric-fronted, and an easy modification is to swap the seats for leather items from another car or 944.

The constant wear from getting in and out of the car tends to fray the fabric/leatherette on the driver's RHS bolster, and the seams connecting the fabric to the leatherette tend to give way, showing the foam underneath. Regrettably, this isn't as simple or cheap to repair as many sellers would have you believe, and requires a replacement piece of fabric to be sewn into the seat by a car trimmer.

Standard seat in pasha trim.

All fabric-fronted seat from 924S Le Mans.

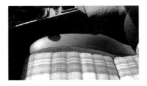

A split seat.

Seats may be raised with Porsche alloy blocks fitted under the runners, and these can make driving the car more comfortable for shorter drivers.

The rear seats are trimmed in the seat fabric with a leatherette centre. They fold to increase the available boot (trunk) space. Front inertia reel seatbelts and optional rear inertia or fixed seat belts were available.

Carpets

Carpets are pre-moulded by Porsche and fit snugly. Their biggest weakness is fading, and looking unsightly. Being nylon, they don't respond well to dyeing, although there are proprietary techniques that claim to restore the original colour. Replacement carpets aren't available new from Porsche, although good quality secondhand items can be found for a reasonable price through breakers or on internet auction sites. For owners in the USA, look at www.stockinteriors.com which advertises replacement *moulded* carpet sets.

Lift footmats, if present, to check for wear and tear, especially in the driver's footwell. Checking for dampness is one way to determine if the car leaks.

Headlining/sunroof

The headlining is made of vinyl and can come unstuck at the rear of the cabin roof, next to the rear hatch. Repairs are fairly easy and inexpensive.

If the optional sunroof is fitted to the car – and many cars have this excellent feature – check that the catches work correctly and the condition of the sunroof seal. The sunroof drainage channels, if blocked, could account for leaks in the front footwells. The roof lifts out of the car and has a specially designed bag, which hangs from the rear hatch hinges, to prevent it being damaged. Once removed, it fits between the wheelarches in the rear of the car. Check that the bag is available. Many are sold separately for extra profit, and – exceptionally – a cargo net was also an option to secure the roof and other luggage from moving around in the rear of the car. The sunroof should be trouble-free in a well-maintained car. The 924S model sunroof can be electrically tilted, or removed.

Sunroof removed.

Sunroof bag in stowed position.

Dashboard

The dash is often referred to as a 'square dash' (the shape of the instrument cowl is square-ish) to differentiate it from the later model 944 dashes, which were called 'oval.' A small glovebox is found on the passenger side: check that the vinyl at the bottom of the glovebox lid isn't lifting.

Dashboards are made of vinyl stretched over a compacted cardboard. Unfortunately, in the sun,

'Square' dash.

30

Glovebox vinyl lifting.

Cracked dash.

these materials expand and contract at different rates, which tends to split the vinyl – usually from one or more of the heater holes at the front of the dash, and, in extreme cases, at almost any point on the dashboard. Uncracked examples are very rare, but do exist. This shouldn't put you off buying an otherwise good car, and replacements can occasionally be found on internet auction sites or from breakers. Replacement can be done as a DIY job but is fairly involved and takes many hours.

Door panels ☐4 ☐3 ☐2 ☐1

The door panels are relatively simple affairs with a vinyl top, with the word Porsche embossed on some models. Manual window winders can be found on early models, in the body of the door panel, however, electric windows feature on most models, and the up/down switches are fitted at the front of this top vinyl panel. On the driver's side, the switches to alter the position of the electric wing mirrors can be found. The passenger mirror was an option, but is usually fitted. The switch to toggle between left and right mirrors is found on the centre console. Check the operation of both mirrors.

Fabric-trimmed door panel.

Check the condition of the bottom of the door panel. These are made of a cardboard-like material and can become soggy if rain runs through the door window seal. When the panels dry out, they can expand as the material's layers delaminate and make the door panel and fabric appear uneven, or even separate completely. In really bad cases the bottom of the panel can disintegrate.

Electric mirror adjustment switches.

Door handles & locks ☐4 ☐3 ☐2 ☐1

The finish on door handles can wear and appear tired after 25 plus-years. Replacements are available secondhand.

Tired door handle.

Any purchase should have at least two keys to operate the door locks. Check that both door locks work smoothly and that both keys also undo the rear hatch window. An electric release was an option on late 924 and 924S models. Don't forget to check that the key also operates the lockable filler cap, if the car has one.

Electric windows ☒ ☒ ☒ ☒

Check that both electric windows go down and up smoothly, and make sure that the passenger window works from both the drivers and passengers switches. Unfortunately, electrical gremlins can be present and the motors do sometimes wear out (the grease in the mechanism hardens, making the motor work harder and eventually burn out). If you buy the car, lubricate the window channels with silicon spray, as this aids the window's movement and reduces the load on the motors.

Electric window switches.

Steering wheel ☒ ☒ ☒ ☒

Early cars have a three-spoke leather-trimmed steering wheel, with 1981-onwards cars having four spokes. Non-standard steering wheels detract from the originality of the car, and if the diameter is significantly smaller, the rim can mask the instrument dials from the driver. Steering column stalks operate the wipers and the lights, and were metal in early cars, replaced by plastic in later models. Check their operation in all positions.

Three-spoke steering wheel.

Instrument panel ☒ ☒ ☒ ☒

Instruments in 924s consist of three main dials in front of the driver and three smaller dials in the centre console. Occasionally, odometers (mileometers) can break. Earlier cars had green numbers and letters on the dial, whereas later cars had white. Switchgear for hazard lights and heated rear window are to the left of the steering column, with the headlight switch to the right. These switches can sometimes fail, but can be found easily secondhand.

Four-spoke steering wheel.

The centre console has three dials at the top (oil pressure, clock, and voltmeter). Check that the oil pressure at start-up is five to six bar, and at least two to three bar when running. Be wary if the pressure falls below one bar. If the oil sender unit fails, the oil pressure will show as five bar as soon as the ignition key is turned on.

Instrument panel and console instruments.

At the rear of the centre console, facing towards the dash, are four smaller toggle switches for: 1) choosing which mirror to adjust; 2) activating the headlamp washer (when the headlamps are on); 3) rear wash wiper; and, 4) foglamps. Check

Armrest/cassette holder.

that all these switches work as, again, electrical issues can arise. Check also the operation of the heater and associated fans.

An optional armrest/cassette holder is sometimes fitted, and is held by four screws through the transmission tunnel. Check that the plastic hinge isn't broken.

Air-conditioning

If fitted, check that the air coming from the internal vents is ice-cold in operation. Check when the unit was last serviced, and the refrigerant used. Anything other than R134A refrigerant should be changed as soon as possible by a certificated air-conditioning specialist, and this needs to be factored into the purchase price.

Gearsticks and 'boxes

Early cars have four-speed 'H' pattern layouts. From 1978, 924s and later 924Ss have a traditional five-speed layout (fifth gear to the right and up). The 924 Turbo and the Carreras, however, have a 'dogleg' first gear. This means that first is to the left and down, leaving the standard 'H' pattern for second to fifth gears. This racing-derived layout can take a bit of getting used to, but becomes second nature after a little practice. US 924 Turbos received a normal pattern gearbox for 1981 cars.

Handbrake

The handbrake on RHD 924s is found by the driver's seat on the right-hand side, and on LHD cars by the driver's seat on the left-hand side.

It's cable operated with small pads gripping the inside of the rear brake disc bell (or drum). Check the handbrake operation as well as the travel, to make sure the cable isn't stretched.

Boot (trunk) blind, hiding contents.

Rear of car

The rear seats are rarely used so the material should be in good condition. Check that the retaining catches work and that the seats fold down easily. On the back of the rear seats is a pull-out roller blind, which hides items left in the boot (trunk) from prying eyes. Check the operation and condition of the blind and ensure it retracts easily.

Spacesaver spare tyre compressor.

Under the boot carpet is rubber-backed sound proofing, which should still be in one piece. The spare wheel is carried in a separate well at the back of the car. Many cars have a spacesaver spare wheel, designed to be pumped up in an emergency by a small compressor which plugs into the car's cigarette lighter. Check that this is present, if appropriate. Lift out the spare wheel and check for corrosion underneath. 924 tool kits are fairly basic and should be found in the spare wheel well with the jack.

To either side of the car at the rear are separate storage wells. Check these, too, for corrosion.

Check also for signs of accident damage in the floor of the boot. Any signs of welding, ripples, or fresh paint should be investigated thoroughly.

Rear side storage well.

Condition of seals   ▢4 ▢3 ▢2 ▢1

Check the condition of the seals around the rear screen, the doors, and the sunroof. They should spring back when compressed, and should not be dry and cracked.

Lift the rear carpet (as described above) as well as the front carpets if possible (but certainly any floor mats) to check for dampness which would indicate a seal or drainage channel is blocked. Dampness in the nearside footwell can also be caused by a loose grommet under the nearside wing, where the aerial wires pass into the car.

Lift carpets to examine front footwells.

Check the soundproofing under the bonnet (hood).

Engine compartment   ▢4 ▢3 ▢2 ▢1

Bear in mind that the 2.0-litre engines in the 924 and 924 Turbo are different to that in the 2.5-litre 924S (which has PORSCHE cast into the rocker cover). How clean and tidy is the engine? Is everything well cared for, or dirty, grimy and rusty? Are oil leaks clearly visible? Is the under bonnet soundproofing in good condition? Are the belts in good condition?

What is the condition of the wiring and terminals; is it neat and tidy with the insulation tape in place (especially important where wires pass near the hot exhaust, which can melt the insulation and possibly cause a fire)? Pull off a few terminals to check that they aren't corroded. Check chassis legs for signs of a previous accident. Check the wing bolts, too, to see if they are original or whether the car has had new wings. The model name should be shown on a decal on the engine bay RHS inner wing.

Check the engine number and the chassis number as described in chapter 7.

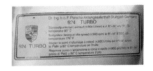
Model name, on decal on engine bay RHS wing.

Fluids   ▢4 ▢3 ▢2 ▢1

Start by looking at the oil, which should be brown (the lighter the better), not thick and black. Check as a guide to when the car was last serviced. For 924 Turbos, check that a fully synthetic oil is being used, as close to 20:50 weight as possible, to protect the turbo bearings.

Check the brake and clutch fluid reservoirs; are they fresh looking and topped up, with no leaks visible? When were the fluids last changed?

Undo the oil filler cap on the top of the rocker cover and check that it's 'oily.' Any trace of a white mayonnaise-like substance indicates possible head gasket issues. 924S models occasionally have a faulty seal in the integral oil cooler, which results in the mixing of oil and coolant and can be misdiagnosed as a head gasket problem.

The service history should back up the seller's answers. If this isn't available, form your own view, asking an expert if you aren't sure of what to look for.

Cooling system ④ ③ ② ①

Check coolant hose condition.

Check the condition of the hoses under the bonnet (hood). Are they hard and brittle, or flexible and in good condition? Ensure there are no cracks or splits. Check the radiator for stone damage, and the lower oil cooler and hoses where fitted. Start the car and check that the cooling fans come on when the engine temperature rises above its normal operating temperature, as thermostats have been known to fail. Occasionally, the coolant temperature sensor washer can leak.

Ensure the coolant has been changed as recommended: regular changes using the correct ratio of anti-freeze to water protects the engine from corrosion. Check the coolant's colour and smell: it should be fresh, bright (most anti-freeze is coloured with fluorescent dye), and not foul-smelling.

Battery ④ ③ ② ①

Check the age and condition of the battery, and that it's the correct rating for the car (53Ah, or uprated to 60 or 63Ah). Does it turn over the car easily? Check the terminals for a build-up of crystals evidencing poor maintenance. Also check that battery acid hasn't corroded the battery tray and bodywork underneath the battery, as in extreme cases this will allow water to enter the nearside footwell and can soak the fusebox.

On normally-aspirated cars, check the condition of the heavy wire that connects the battery with the starter motor. This passes close to the extremely hot exhaust, which can melt the insulation, causing the wire to short on the exhaust.

Braking system ④ ③ ② ①

Brake master cylinder and servo.

Early 924s have front disc brakes and rear drum brakes. Most models, however, have servo-assisted disc brakes front and rear. You'll already have checked the brake fluid condition, and asked when it was changed, when carrying out the fluid checks, but now check the reservoir and brake servo condition (under the bonnet): any evidence of dampness on the

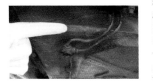

Check the brake pipes.

servo housing suggests a leak which should be investigated immediately. Check the condition of the master cylinder seals, and the brake lines which run from it, for corrosion. The brake lines under the body should be checked to all four callipers, especially where they bend.

Check all four callipers to ensure that the pistons aren't sticking, and check the discs for wear, noting the size of lip at the outer edge, or any scoring, cracking or pitting. Check the pads for wear.

Clutch

Check that the pedal operation is smooth. Normally-aspirated 924s have a cable operated clutch. 924T and S models have hydraulic clutches: if the flexible pipe from the clutch master cylinder to the rigid pipe joining the clutch slave cylinder fails, it can act as a one way valve, causing the clutch pedal to stick when changing gear.

Check that the heater matrix valve, situated just above the clutch housing, isn't leaking, as this will allow coolant to contaminate the clutch, or corrode the roller bearings in the spigot bearing at the end of the crankshaft. This evidences itself as poor synchromesh operation or the impression that the clutch is binding. It's good practice to change these roller bearings each time the clutch is changed.

Windscreen/windshield washer systems

924s have two washer systems; the front windscreen (operated from the steering column stalks) and the headlamp washers (operated from the four small switches). Check that both work.

Engine bay leaks

In 924s, engine leaks typically occur around the cam seal and/or rocker cover; in 924Ts around the crankcase, and are normally breather issues. In the 924S models, leaks typically occur around the front engine oil seals. A leak at the front of the 924S exhaust manifold is usually caused by a leaking O-ring between the cam tower and the rear cam pulley cover. Check all hoses for leaks.

Engine mountings

Hard to see even when on a ramp, but check, where possible, that the rubber hasn't perished. If the car vibrates badly at idle, and these vibrations disappear at around 1200–1500 revs, the engine mounts may be to blame.

The 924S right-hand engine mount sometimes collapses, due to being too near to the extremely hot exhaust manifold. You can diagnose this from the bottom screw on the distributor cap; it should be above the headlamp bar – if it's level or lower, the exhaust side engine mount has sagged.

Fuel-injection system

The 924 series uses a Bosch K-jetronic mechanical fuel system, which normally causes few, if any, problems. Remove the rubber butterfly valve housing and check that the plate isn't oily, which might point to a collapsed breather pipe or dirty throttle body (this can cause the car to stall when slowing down, at junctions for instance). Check the condition of the metal pipes leading to the injectors, looking for corrosion, and check that the flexible fuel pipes leading

K-Jetronic metering head.

to the metering unit haven't perished. If you purchase the car, it's often worth using a good injector cleaner occasionally.

Exhaust system ④ ③ ② ①
The exhaust system uses a cast iron manifold which can occasionally split (but can be welded or replaced secondhand). The rest of the system is steel and corrodes, so check the condition. With the engine running, put your hand over the end of the exhaust for a few seconds, and listen for any blowing noises. It can be difficult to find original (or even pattern) parts for some models, but specialists can normally assist.

Steering box/rack ④ ③ ② ①
Check the top universal joint, and those underneath, for excess play, and make sure that the steering movements are smooth.

Power steering pump/reservoir ④ ③ ② ①
Relates mainly to the 924S. Check the reservoir fluid level, and that the fluid is a light red colour, with no black flecks in it. The steering should be smooth with no judder. Check there are no leaks from the power assisted steering pump (evidenced by a groaning noise).

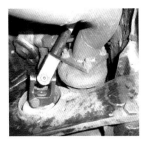

Steering universal joint (UJ), located next to the turbocharger.

Turbocharger ④ ③ ② ①
Ideally, after a fast run, the car should be left idling for a minute or so, to allow oil to cool the turbo bearings, prolonging the life of the turbo. Should the owner switch the car off immediately after a spirited run, turbo life will more than likely be reduced. Typically, turbos are good for some 40,000 miles, however some last far longer than this if treated properly.

Test the hub bearings.

Hub bearings and steering joints ④ ③ ② ①
If possible, jack up the car so the wheels are off the ground (front first, then rear). Holding the top and bottom of the tyre, pull and push the wheel to feel for excess play. Top/bottom play indicates a worn shock absorber or lower balljoint. Side-to-side play indicates a worn trackrod or trackrod end. Play in both directions can also indicate wheel bearing issues.

Suspension ④ ③ ② ①
Check that each shock absorber isn't leaking fluid, and that the springs aren't broken (a leaking/tired shock absorber or broken spring will cause one corner of the car to droop). Replacements, if needed, are readily available at reasonable cost.

Brakes

[4] [3] [2] [1]

Check the look of the brakes; are the discs shiny and smooth, or rusty, pitted or cracked? Before the road test (they get very hot afterwards), run your finger across the disc and feel for a lip at the outer edge representing the amount of wear. Check the thickness of the pads next to the disc by looking at the amount of lining left (at least 5mm is recommended). Check when the fluid was last replaced (every two years is recommended), and verify this from the service history, if possible. Check that the callipers haven't seized, especially in a car that has been standing for a while.

Early cars have rear drum brakes. Again, check when last inspected, and how much lining is left on the shoes, if possible. If this isn't possible to do during your 60 minute inspection, have them checked as soon as possible after the purchase.

The handbrake works against the bell of the rear discs, or against the drum on early cars. The handbrake lever should pull up three or four notches. These rarely give any major problems.

Check the master cylinder under the bonnet isn't leaking (shown by a stain on the servo behind the master cylinder).

Gearbox

[4] [3] [2] [1]

Early 924s have a four-speed gearbox (plus reverse). A five forward speed option became available in 1978, and was standard on the 924 Turbo and 924S.

Gear changes need to be deliberate, but should be quiet and easy – although many 924s (especially Turbos) have a worn synchromesh on first gear (and sometimes second), making it hard to engage these gears whilst moving. High mileage cars can suffer from bearing wear, manifesting itself as a whine that increases in frequency as the car increases its speed. If the car has an automatic gearbox, with the engine running, check that the fluid is a bright, fresh-smelling red colour with no black flecks in it.

Rear axle

[4] [3] [2] [1]

This contains the gearbox and differential on 924s (called a transaxle layout, giving better weight distribution). Check the oil's condition and level in the gearbox, and check when last changed (an indicator of a well maintained car). Check there are no oil leaks

Transaxle at rear of car.

from the transaxle output shaft seals, and that the rubber covers over the two constant velocity joints on each of the driveshafts have not split.

Constant velocity (CV) joint cover.

An option of a limited-slip differential (LSD) was also available on Turbo/CGT models, and is often found on European cars in countries where the winters are particularly cold.

Test drive (minimum 15 minutes)

[4] [3] [2] [1]

Hopefully, the seller will already have started the car for you (as described in chapter 7), so you will have a basic idea of how the car runs. Now, if possible, ask the seller if you can drive the car (and take your certificate of insurance to prove you have al least third party cover). Coloured smoke is an issue: on a 924T, blue smoke at idle, that disappears on acceleration, is likely to be a turbo oil leak into the compressor side of the turbo, while blue smoke on acceleration is likely to be a piston ring issue. White smoke at idle is likely to be a head gasket issue or a turbo oil leak into the exhaust side of the turbo. Also, listen to the exhaust; is it blowing?

Check that all the dash warning lights come on at ignition, but all go out on starting the car, and that all the everyday controls work, and the headlights raise.

Most models don't have power steering, so expect the steering to be heavy at low speeds, but very direct in action (ie, no vagueness when turning). The car should pull well without any strange noises, and not pull to either side when driven.

Try all the gears during the drive. Gear changes should be quiet and easy, although a worn synchromesh on first gear, and sometimes second, will make it hard to engage these gears whilst moving, or cause graunching if not double-declutched. This is an expensive fix. Check, also, that reverse engages cleanly.

The clutch should bite shortly after the pedal is lifted, and not at the top of its travel (indicating an expensive clutch replacement will be needed shortly). If in doubt, try starting the car in third gear and see if the clutch slips. On 924Ss, if it's hard to select gears and the car lurches after engaging the clutch, or 'clonks' on accelerating or overrun, it's usually the rubber centre of the clutch failing.

Where a turbo is fitted, during the test drive the turbo should 'spool up' at around 2500-3000 revs, and produce impressive acceleration to around 5500 revs. A 'zinging' feeling through the foot when accelerating is often a sign that the engine mountings are tired.

A 'ghostly' hum at around 40mph signifies wheel bearing problems. A rattling noise (like a stone in a brake drum) from the rear when the clutch is depressed can indicate a failing torque tube.

Ensure that all the brakes work smoothly without juddering, and that they stop the car in a straight line without fading. Check the handbrake works by applying it on a hill, or trying (gently) to pull away with the handbrake applied.

The steering should lighten as speed increases, and shouldn't pull or veer to one side or the other. The steering should be direct with no feeling of vagueness. 'Clunks' on cornering indicate possible suspension problems.

Listen for unwanted noises – whines, rumbles, knocking noises – all of which will need further investigation.

Check the centre console oil pressure gauge and voltmeter. At start-up, the oil pressure should be five to six bar falling, to two to three bar when the car warms up. The voltmeter should show a reading of just under 14 volts when the car is running.

The water temperature gauge, in the three main dash instruments, should settle to a constant reading as the car warms up, and rise when the car is stationary to the point where the fan cuts in to reduce the temperature. This is an easy way to check the operation of the fan and confirm the cooling system is working.

Check that all the lights, wipers (including the intermittent facility) and washers and switches work.

If the car has a rare automatic gearbox, check that it changes up and down smoothly through all the gears.

If possible, carry out a ramp check (many exhaust/tyre centres will let you put a car on a ramp for fifteen minutes or so, for a small fee), and check the following:
• Floorpan: check for signs of corrosion or accident damage, especially around the sills area

• Fuel tank: check for for signs of leaking (they can weep at the welds)
• Fuel and brake lines: condition, especially around junctions and bends
• Exhaust system and mountings: (most US cars have catalytic converters)
• Suspension, wishbone, castor and roll bar rubber bushes: check for perishing or splitting
• Leaks from under the engine
• Engine mountings condition
• Hoses at the bottom of the engine bay and around the fuel tank
• Check the condition of all the steering rack rubbers, and use a pry bar to test for excess movement in the suspension and steering joints.

Testing the suspension components.

Paperwork/title

You have probably already checked the paperwork as part of the 15 minute evaluation, chapter 7, but do ask to see the list of recommendations and the emissions print out: a readout of 80-200ppm hydrocarbon emissions is average for a sound engine. Lastly, verify the mileage of the vehicle if at all possible.

Evaluation procedure

Add up the total points.

Score: 180 = excellent; 135 = good; 90 = average; 45 = poor.

Cars scoring over 126 will be completely usable and will require only maintenance and care to preserve condition. Cars scoring between 45 and 92 will require some serious work (at much the same cost regardless of score). Cars scoring between 93 and 125 will require very careful assessment of the necessary repair/restoration costs in order to arrive at a realistic value.

10 Auctions
– sold! Another way to buy your dream

924 race car for sale at auction.

Auction pros & cons

Pros: Prices will usually be lower than those of dealers or private sellers, and you might grab a real bargain on the day. Auctioneers have usually established clear title with the seller. At the venue you can usually examine documentation relating to the vehicle.

Cons: You have to rely on a sketchy catalogue description of condition and history. The opportunity to inspect is limited, and you cannot drive the car. Auction cars are often a little below par and may require some work. It's easy to overbid. There will usually be a buyer's premium to pay in addition to the auction hammer price.

Which auction?

Auctions by established auctioneers are advertised in car magazines and on the auction houses' websites. A catalogue, or a simple printed list of the lots for auctions might only be available a day or two ahead, though often lots are listed and pictured on auctioneers' websites much earlier. Contact the auction company to ask if previous auction selling prices are available as this is useful information (details of past sales are often available on websites).

Catalogue, entry fee and payment details
When you purchase the catalogue of the vehicles in the auction, it often acts as a ticket allowing two people to attend the viewing days and the auction. Catalogue details tend to be comparatively brief, but will include information such as 'one owner from new, low mileage, full service history', etc. It will also usually show a guide price to give you some idea of what to expect to pay and will tell you what is charged as a 'Buyer's premium'. The catalogue will also contain details of acceptable forms of payment. At the fall of the hammer an immediate deposit is usually required, the balance payable within 24 hours. If the plan is to pay by cash there may be a cash limit. Some auctions will accept payment by debit card. Sometimes credit or charge cards are acceptable, but will often incur an extra charge. A bank draft or bank transfer will have to be arranged in advance with your own bank as well as with the auction house. No car will be released before all payments are cleared. If delays occur in payment transfers, then storage costs can accrue.

Buyer's premium
A buyer's premium will be added to the hammer price: don't forget this in your calculations. It is not usual for there to be a further state tax or local tax on the purchase price and/or on the buyer's premium.

Viewing
In some instances it's possible to view on the day, or days before, as well as in the hours prior to, the auction. There are auction officials available who are willing to help out by opening engine and luggage compartments and to allow you to inspect the interior. While the officials may start the engine for you, a test drive is out of the question. Crawling under and around the car as much as you want is permitted, but you can't suggest that the car you are interested in be jacked up, or attempt to do the job yourself. You can also ask to see any documentation available.

Bidding
Before you take part in the auction, decide your maximum bid – and stick to it!
It may take a while for the auctioneer to reach the lot you are interested in, so use that time to observe how other bidders behave. When it's the turn of your car, attract the auctioneer's attention and make an early bid. The auctioneer will then look to you for a reaction every time another bid is made, usually the bids will be in fixed increments until the bidding slows, when smaller increments will often be accepted before the hammer falls. If you want to withdraw from the bidding, make sure the auctioneer understands your intentions - a vigorous shake of the head when he or she looks to you for the next bid should do the trick!
Assuming that you are the successful bidder, the auctioneer will note your card or paddle number, and from that moment on you will be responsible for the vehicle.
If the car is unsold, either because it failed to reach the reserve or because there was little interest, it may be possible to negotiate with the owner, via the auctioneers, after the sale is over.

Successful bid

There are two more items to think about. How to get the car home, and insurance. If you can't drive the car, your own or a hired trailer is one way, another is to have the vehicle shipped using the facilities of a local company. The auction house will also have details of companies specialising in the transfer of cars.

Insurance for immediate cover can usually be purchased on site, but it may be more cost-effective to make arrangements with your own insurance company in advance, and then call to confirm the full details.

eBay & other online auctions

eBay & other online auctions could land you a car at a bargain price, though you'd be foolhardy to bid without examining the car first, something most vendors encourage. A useful feature of eBay is that the geographical location of the car is shown, so you can narrow your choices to those within a realistic radius of home. Be prepared to be outbid in the last few moments of the auction. Remember, your bid is binding and that it will be very, very difficult to get restitution in the case of a crooked vendor fleecing you – caveat emptor!

Be aware that some cars offered for sale in online auctions are 'ghost' cars. Don't part with any cash without being sure that the vehicle does actually exist and is as described (usually pre-bidding inspection is possible).

Auctioneers

Barrett-Jackson
www.barrett-jackson.com
Bonhams www.bonhams.com
British Car Auctions (BCA)
www.bca-europe.com or
www.british-car-auctions.co.uk
Cheffins www.cheffins.co.uk

Christies www.christies.com
Coys www.coys.co.uk
eBay www.eBay.com
H&H www.classic-auctions.co.uk
RM www.rmauctions.com
Shannons www.shannons.com.au
Silver www.silverauctions.com

11 Paperwork
– correct documentation is essential!

The paper trail
Porsches usually come with a large portfolio of paperwork accumulated and passed on by a succession of proud owners. This documentation represents the real history of the car and from it can be deduced the level of care the car has received, how much it's been used, which specialists have worked on it and the dates of major repairs and restorations. All of this information will be priceless to you as the new owner, so be very wary of cars with little paperwork to support their claimed history.

Registration documents
All countries/states have some form of registration for private vehicles, whether it's like the American 'pink slip' system or the British 'log book' system.

It's essential to check that the registration document is genuine, that it relates to the car in question, and that all the vehicle's details are correctly recorded, including chassis/VIN and engine numbers (if these are shown). If you're buying from the previous owner, his or her name and address will be recorded in the document: this may not be the case if you're buying from a dealer.

In the UK, the current (Euro-aligned) registration document is named 'V5C' and the front is now principally red. Inside sections relate to the car specification, with a section to advise the DVLA in the UK of the details of a new owner when the car is sold. A small section in yellow deals with selling the car within the motor trade.

In the UK, the DVLA will provide details of earlier keepers of the vehicle upon payment of a small fee, and much can be learned in this way.

If the car has a foreign registration, there may be expensive and time-consuming formalities to complete. Do you really want the hassle?

Roadworthiness certificate
Most country/state administrations require that vehicles are regularly tested to prove that they are safe to use on the public highway, and don't produce excessive emissions. In the UK that test (the 'MoT') is carried out at approved testing stations, for a fee. In the USA the requirement varies, but most states insist on an emissions test every two years as a minimum, while the police are charged with pulling over unsafe-looking vehicles.

In the UK the test is required on an annual basis once a vehicle becomes three years-old. Of particular relevance for older cars, is that the certificate issued includes the mileage reading recorded at the test date and, therefore, becomes an independent record of that car's history. Ask the seller if previous certificates are available. Without an MoT the vehicle should be trailered to its new home, unless you insist that a valid MoT is part of the deal. (Not such a bad idea this, as at least you'll know the car was roadworthy on the day it was tested and you don't need to wait for the old certificate to expire before having the test done.)

Road licence
The administration of every country/state charges some kind of tax for the use of its road system. The actual form of the 'road licence' and how it's displayed varies enormously from country-to-country and state-to-state.

Whatever the form of the 'road licence,' it must relate to the vehicle carrying it and must be present and valid if the car is to be driven on the public highway legally. The value of the licence will depend on the length of time it will continue to be valid.

In the UK, if a car is untaxed because it hasn't been used for a period of time, the owner has to inform the licensing authorities that the vehicle is being kept off the road. Also in the UK, vehicles built before the end of 1972 are provided with 'tax discs' free of charge, but they must still display a valid disc. Car clubs can often provide formal proof that a particular car qualifies for this valuable concession.

Certificates of authenticity
For many makes of collectible car, it's possible to get a certificate proving the age and authenticity (eg, engine and chassis numbers, paint colour and trim) of a particular vehicle, these are sometimes called 'Heritage Certificates,' and if the car comes with one of these, it's a definite bonus. If you want to obtain one, the relevant owners' club is the best starting point.

If the car has been used in European classic car rallies, it may have a FIVA (Federation Internationale des Vehicules Anciens) certificate. The so-called 'FIVA Passport', or 'FIVA Vehicle Identity Card,' enables organisers and participants to recognise whether or not a particular vehicle is suitable for individual events. If you want to obtain such a certificate go to www.fbhvc.co.uk or www.fiva.org, there will be similar organisations in other countries, too.

Valuation certificate
Hopefully, the vendor will have a recent valuation certificate, or letter signed by a recognised expert stating how much he, or she, believes the particular car to be worth (such documents, together with photos, are usually needed to get 'agreed value' insurance). Generally such documents should act only as confirmation of your own assessment of the car, rather than a guarantee of value, as the expert has probably not seen the car in the flesh. The easiest way to find out how to obtain a formal valuation is to contact the owners' club.

Service history
Often, 924s will have been serviced at home by enthusiastic (and hopefully capable) owners for a good number of years. Nevertheless, try to obtain as much service history and other paperwork pertaining to the car as you can. Naturally, dealer stamps, or specialist garage receipts score most points in the value stakes. However, anything helps in the great authenticity game, items like the original bill of sale, handbook, parts invoices and repair bills, adding to the story and the character of the car. Even a brochure correct to the year of the car's manufacture is a useful document and something that you could well have to search hard to locate in future years. If the seller claims that the car has been restored, then expect receipts and other evidence from a specialist restorer.

If the seller claims to have carried out regular servicing, ask what work was completed, when, and seek some evidence of it being carried out. Your assessment of the car's overall condition should tell you whether the seller's claims are genuine.

Restoration photographs
If the seller tells you that the car has been restored, then expect to be shown a series of photographs taken while the restoration was under way. Pictures taken at

A 924 during restoration.

various stages, and from various angles, should help you gauge the thoroughness of the work. If you buy the car, ask if you can have all the photographs, as they form an important part of the vehicle's history. It's surprising how many sellers are happy to part with their car and accept your cash, but want to hang on to their photographs! In the latter event, you may be able to persuade the vendor to let you get a set of copies made.

12 What's it worth?

– let your head rule your heart

Condition

If the car you've been looking at is really bad, then you've probably not bothered to use the marking system in chapter 9 – 60 minute evaluation. You may not have even got as far as using that chapter at all! If you did use the marking system, you'll know whether the car is in Excellent (maybe Concours), Good, Average, or Poor condition or, perhaps, somewhere in-between these categories.

Many car magazines run a regular price guide. If you haven't bought the latest editions, do so now and compare their suggested values for the model you're thinking of buying: also look at the auction prices they're reporting. Values have been fairly stable for some time, but some models will always be more sought-after than others. Trends can change too. The values published in the magazines tend to vary from one magazine to another, as do their scales of condition, so read carefully the guidance notes they provide. Bear in mind that a car that is truly a recent show winner could be worth more than the highest scale published. Assuming that the car you have in mind is not in show/concours condition, then relate the level of condition that you judge the car to be in with the appropriate guide price. How does the figure compare with the asking price? Before you start haggling with the seller, consider what affect any variation from standard specification might have on the car's value. If you are buying from a dealer, remember there will be a dealer's premium on the price.

Desirable options/extras

Many 924s were ordered with the removable sunroof option, which gives the car a 'Targa' like feel when stowed in the rear. The associated sunroof bag and straps are most useful, as is the cargo net option for stopping items moving around in the rear of the car.

Standard 924s often add a 924 Turbo spoiler, which enhances the look, and full leather trim looks superb and is generally harder wearing than the leatherette and fabric. The transmission tunnel armrest (originally designed to hold cassette tapes) provides a useful resting place for one's elbow.

A limited-slip differential is a rare but useful option for giving better control when driving in a spirited manner. Air-conditioning is a useful option too, but adds considerable weight. Check which refrigerant is used (see chapter 9).

Undesirable features

An automatic gearbox blunts performance. Non-original steering wheels and gearknobs detract from the originality of a vehicle, as do non-Porsche road wheels.

Beware of poor resprays (or cars needing an expensive respray) and cars with poor interiors. See chapter 7 for the common problem areas to avoid.

Striking a deal

Negotiate on the basis of your condition assessment, mileage and fault rectification cost. To a lesser extent, also take into account the car's specification. Be realistic about the value, but don't be completely intractable: a small compromise on the part of the vendor or buyer will often facilitate a deal at little real cost.

Restoration seems such a good idea when one sees a restored car, however, let's be realistic about what is actually involved.

A superbly restored fast road 924 Turbo, amidst other exotica.

A rolling restoration allows you to enjoy your 924 whilst improving one area at a time, as funds allow. The finished result is unlikely to be as impressive as a full 'nut and bolt' effort, but the stress will also be much reduced!

If funds allow, you might consider a professional restoration. Professional restorers usually have more than one employee, and can restore your car in months rather than years. The high cost is unlikely to be warranted when looking

The same car during restoration.

at the value of the finished car in anything other than, perhaps, a 924 Carrera GTS or GTR. Do check finished examples of the restorer's work for quality and finish before spending your money – doing it twice will hurt at least twice as much!

A DIY restoration, like most things in life, has pros and cons.

Pros. The satisfaction of creating a 'better than new' car from a tired example. Lots of new skills and techniques to learn. Hours of fun!

Still fancy a restoration?

Cons. Time: do you have the uncommitted time to spend (usually evenings and weekends) for what may be a number of years? Money: restoration is not cheap. Whilst you may not have labour costs, new parts, trim, respraying, etc, will add up to many thousands of pounds. Typically, set budgets are woefully inadequate.

Skills. Do you have the necessary skills to take a car apart and then put it back together? Have you restored a car before?

Space. Ideally, you'll need a large garage or workshop, allowing you to store the many items that come off your car whilst working on other parts. Engines, doors, glass, seats, carpets, etc, all take up lots of room when not in a car.

Support. Does your partner understand the tremendous effort required, and are they prepared to support you as you disappear into the garage every evening and weekend?

Knowledge. Do you know to whom work can be subbed-out? Experience of reasonably priced, good quality tradesmen is invaluable (club contacts can probably assist).

Dedication. It takes a lot of drive to leave a warm living room, after dinner in the depths of winter, and work for several hours in a cold garage.

Value. Is the finished article something you want to keep? Selling it will undoubtedly not recoup the money spent on restoration.

In summary, restoring a 924 as a hobby, recognising the risks, will net you a wonderful car that will give lifelong service. However, don't start a restoration unless you are sure you'll finish it.

There are two schools of thought regarding the condition of car you should buy to restore. A tatty non-runner will be inexpensive, but, typically, everything will need refurbishing. A good but tired car will cost more, but may need less spending on it overall and may be easier to work on. "You pay your money and make your choice."

14 Paint problems
– bad complexion, including dimples, pimples and bubbles

Generally speaking, corrosion isn't as major an issue with 924s as it is with many other cars of the 1970s and 1980s, as the bodies were galvanised at the factory when the cars were built. Regrettably, the paint finish tends not to fare as well, and if not properly looked after during its life, or due to accident damage or poor preparation prior to a respray, any of the following problems may be seen.

Orange peel
This appears as an uneven paint surface, similar to the appearance of the skin of an orange. The fault is caused by the failure of atomized paint droplets to flow into each other when they hit the surface. It's sometimes possible to rub out the effect with proprietary paint cutting/rubbing compound, or very fine grades of abrasive paper. A respray may be necessary in severe cases. Consult a bodywork repairer/paint shop for advice on the particular car.

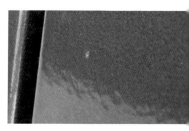

Orange peel.

Cracking
Severe cases are likely to have been caused by too heavy an application of paint (or filler beneath the paint). Also, insufficient stirring of the paint before application can lead to the components being improperly mixed, and cracking can result. Incompatibility with the paint already on the panel can have a similar effect. To rectify the problem it is necessary to rub down to a smooth, sound finish before respraying the problem area.

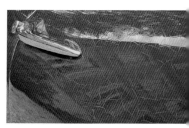

Cracking.

Crazing
Sometimes the paint takes on a crazed rather than a cracked appearance, when the problems mentioned under 'Cracking' are present. This problem can also be caused by a reaction between the underlying surface and the paint. Paint removal and respraying the problem area is usually the only solution.

Blistering
Almost always caused by corrosion of the metal beneath the paint. Usually perforation will be found in the metal and the damage will be worse than that suggested by the area of blistering. The metal will have to be repaired before repainting.

Blistering.

Micro blistering

Usually the result of an economy respray, where inadequate heating has allowed moisture to settle on the car before spraying. Consult a paint specialist, but usually damaged paint will have to be removed before a partial or full respray. Can also be caused by car covers that don't 'breathe.'

Micro blistering.

Fading

Some colours, especially reds, are prone to fading if subjected to strong sunlight for long periods without the benefit of polish protection. Sometimes, proprietary paint restorers and/or paint cutting/rubbing compounds will retrieve the situation. Often a respray is the only real solution.

Fading paint.

Peeling

Often a problem with metallic paintwork when the sealing laquer becomes damaged and begins to peel off. Poorly applied paint may also peel. The remedy is to strip and start again.

Dimples

Dimples in the paintwork are caused by the residue of polish (particularly silicone types) not being removed properly before respraying. Paint removal and repainting is the only solution.

Dents

Small dents are usually easily cured by the 'Dentmaster,' or equivalent process, that sucks or pushes out the dent (as

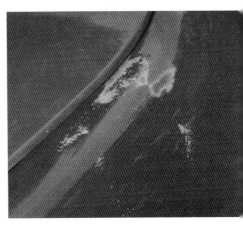
Peeling paint.

long as the paint surface is still intact). Companies offering dent removal services usually come to your home: consult your telephone directory or the internet.

15 Problems due to lack of use
– just like their owners, 924s need exercise!

Ideally, a 924 will be driven at least once a week. If a car hasn't been used for a long period of time (months or even years), it will need looking at in great detail to ensure some of the problems highlighted below have not occurred, as putting these right can potentially be very expensive.

Seized components
Pistons in callipers, slave and master cylinders can seize.

The clutch may seize if the plate becomes stuck to the flywheel because of corrosion. Pumping the pedal or rocking the car may free it.

Handbrakes (parking brakes) can seize if the cables and linkages rust.

Pistons can seize in the bores due to corrosion.

Fluids
Old, acidic oil can corrode bearings. Check the colour of the oil – light brown is a good sign; black or thick black oil is a concern.

Uninhibited coolant can corrode internal waterways. Lack of antifreeze can cause core plugs to be pushed out, and even cracks in the block or head. Silt settling and solidifying can cause overheating.

Brake and clutch fluids absorb water from the atmosphere and should be renewed every two years. Old fluid with a high water content can cause corrosion and pistons/callipers to seize (freeze), and can cause brake failure when the water turns to vapour near hot braking components,

Tyre problems
Tyres that have had the weight of the car on them in a single position for some time will develop flat spots, resulting in some (usually temporary) vibration. The tyre walls may have cracks or blister-type bulges, meaning new tyres are needed.

Shock absorbers (dampers)
With lack of use, the dampers will lose their elasticity or even seize. Creaking, groaning, and stiff suspension are signs of this.

A flat spot in the making.

Rear shock absorbers – old and new.

Rubber and plastic
Radiator hoses may have perished and split, possibly resulting in the loss of all coolant. Window and door seals can harden and leak. Gaitors/boots can crack. Wiper blades will harden.

Electrics
The battery will be of little use if it has not been charged for many months.
    Earthing/grounding problems are common when the connections have corroded. Old bullet- and spade-type electrical connectors commonly rust/corrode and will need disconnecting, cleaning and protection (eg Vaseline).
    Sparkplugs will often have corroded in an unused engine.
    Wiring insulation can harden and fail.

Rotting exhaust system
Exhaust gas contains a high water content so exhaust systems corrode very quickly from the inside when the car is not used.

16 The Community
– key people, organisations and companies in the 924 world

Porsche has been a hugely successful sports car manufacturer for a number of decades, and whilst there have been economic pressures during this time, the key families (Porsche and Piech), through a combination of motorsport victories, design, and price, have maintained the brand value and desirability of their products.

A 924 owners' club rally.

Clubs

Within the UK, the main clubs that support the 924 are:

Porsche Club GB

The largest of the UK clubs with a membership of over 16,000 people. The annual subscription entitles members to a monthly glossy magazine-styled *Porsche Post,* containing topical articles, register columns, and regional reports. Club members obtain discounts off many goods and services, enjoy factory visits, and dedicated race series.

PCGB can be contacted on +44 (0) 1608 652911 or by email at cluboffice@ porscheclubgb.com

The Independent Porsche Enthusiasts Club (TIPEC)

Smaller than PCGB, yet still offering the chance to meet like minded Porsche owners, whatever model owned. Subscriptions are slightly cheaper and offer a bi-monthly magazine, *All Torque*, regional meetings and events, plus a wide array of discounts.

TIPEC can be contacted by email at membership@tipec.net

The 924 Owners' Club

The only club dedicated to the 924 models. A relatively new club, formed in 2005, and specialising in the 924 in all its guises. Again, a friendly welcome awaits new 924 members, with a more modest membership fee providing access to the online help forum, discounts off many goods and services, a number of events throughout the UK, and a bi-monthly magazine *TwoFour*.

The 924 Owners' Club can be contacted by email at membership@ porsche924.co.uk

Outside the UK, there are a number of international Porsche clubs enjoyed by well over 100,000 members worldwide. Here are a few internet addresses. If your country isn't mentioned, search the internet for 'Porsche club <your country>' for details of your local contact.

Porsche Club of America (including Canada)

www.pca.org

www.porsche-club-deutschland.de

This comprises of a number of clubs in different states, eg, Queensland: www.
porsche-qld.org.au

www.porsche.org.nz

Porsche's UK agents. Bath Road, Calcot, Reading, Berkshire RG31 7SE. Telephone
+44 (0) 8457 911911 www.porsche.co.uk

Motorsport
Porsches made their name in motorsport, and it's fitting that the various Clubs
around the world still organise everything from track days to one model race series.
For details of motorsport events in your country, contact your local Porsche
club.

Specialists
The UK 924 specialist who advised on many of the technical aspects covered in this
book is JMG, Unit 1, Station Approach, Fairmile Road, Christchurch, Dorset BH23
2LJ. +44 (0) 1202 488800 www.jmgarage.com
Official Porsche Centres (OPC) have access to the entire parts stock held by
Porsche in Germany, and can get parts within a few days if in stock.
There are independent specialists that can help source parts, and searching the
web can usually help find even the most obscure parts secondhand.

Workshop manuals
See details in chapter 2 – Cost considerations.
There is also a number of online forums which cover the 924 and helpful articles are
available to assist the home mechanic in keeping these excellent cars on the road.

Useful reference books
Porsche 924
    Brian Long, ISBN 9781901295856
The Porsche 924/944 Book
    Peter Morgan, ISBN 9781859608647
Porsche 924.928.944 The new Generation
    Jerry Sloniger, ISBN 9780850454154
Porsche 924, 944, and 968: A Collector's Guide
    Michael Cotton, ISBN 9781899870479
Porsche 924 Gold Portfolio
    A collection of magazine articles. www.brooklandsbooks.com
Original Porsche 924/944/968
    Peter Morgan, ISBN 9781901432053

17 Vital statistics
– essential data at your fingertips

Numbers built

924	122,304
924 Turbo	12,385
924 Carrera GT	400 (+6 prototypes)
924 Carrera GTS	59
924 Carrera GTR	17 (genuine verified)
924S	16,282
Total build numbers	151,447

Performance figures (European)

Model	Bhp	0-62mph	Top speed (mph)	Original price (UK)	Year
924	125	10.5	125	12,123 (Lux)	1985
924 Turbo	170/177	7.8	140	13,998	1981
924 Carrera GT	210	6.9	150	19,211	1980
924 Carrera GTS	245/280	6.2/5.2	155/160+	23,950/31,522	1981
924 Carrera GTR	to 375	4.7	181	39,130	1981
924S	150/160	8.5	133	17,484	1987

Summary of model specifications

924

Capacity: 1984cc water cooled four-cylinder. Steering: rack and pinion. Turning circle: 30.3ft (9.24m). Brakes: twin-circuit hydraulic with diagonal split, servo assisted, disc front, drum rear. Wheels: steel 5.5Jx14 or alloy 6Jx14, with 4 stud fixing. Tyres: steel rims: 165 HR14; alloy rims: 185/70 HR14.
    Dimensions: Length: 166in (4216mm). Width: 66.4in (1687mm). Height: 50in (1270mm). Fuel tank capacity: 13.8 gallons (62.7 litres). Weight: 2380lb (1080kg).

924 Turbo (differences from 924)

Compression: Europe 7.5:1 (later raised to 8.5:1in 1981) with redesigned aluminium alloy crossflow cylinder head. Dog-leg five-speed gearbox. Turbocharger: KKK turbocharger (with wastegate limiting boost to 0.65bar). Fuel system: electric fuel pump (plus second pump in tank) with Bosch K-Jetronic fuel-injection. Brakes: four wheel ventilated discs with Porsche 928 callipers. Wheels: alloy 6Jx15, with 5 stud fixing (optional 16in

924 engine bay.

924 Turbo engine bay.

928 style available 1982). Tyres: alloy rims: 185/70 VR15 (205/55 VR16).

Fuel tank capacity: 13.8 gallons (62 litres); from 1981, 18.5 gallons (84 litres).

Exterior: integrated rear tailgate spoiler. NACA duct in bonnet (hood). Four additional cooling vents in front panel, between headlamps. Additional vents in front valance. Turbo badging on rear panel and sills. Rear wiper as standard.

Weight: 2602lb (1180kg)

924 Carrera GT (differences from 924 and 924 Turbo – see chapter 7)

Turbocharger: KKK turbocharger (with wastegate limiting boost to 0.75bar). Intercooler: air-to-air, mounted under bonnet (hood) air scoop. Brakes: larger brake discs with divided brake circuits. Wheels: forged 'Fuchs' 7Jx15 (optional 7/8Jx16in). Tyres: 215/60 VR15 (205/55 VR16 front/225/50 VR16 rear). Optional limited-slip differential. Fuel tank capacity: 18.5 gallons (84 litres).

Dimensions: length: 170.2in (4320mm). Width: 68.4in (1735mm). Weight: 2602lb (1180kg)

924 Carrera GT engine bay.

924 Carrera GT wings and airscoop.

924 Carrera GT interior (with non-standard steering wheel).

924 Carrera GTS (differences from 924 Carrera GT – individual cars may differ)

Turbocharger: KKK turbocharger with wastegate limiting boost to 1.0bar. Intercooler: air-to-air, mounted at front of car. Brakes: larger 911 Turbo callipers with cross drilled, ventilated brake discs. Wheels: forged 'Fuchs' 8Jx16in. Tyres: 225/50 VR 16. Suspension: cast rear trailing arms and coil springs (replacing torsion bars). 40 per cent Limited-slip differential.

924 Carrera GTS engine bay.

Exterior: (note: some differences exist between cars where customers specified different fittings). Integrated larger rear tailgate spoiler. Revised front spoiler and wings made of fibreglass. GTS motif incorporated into rear panel under rear spoiler. Plexiglass light covers replace pop up headlights. Plexiglass side windows. Fibreglass bonnet.

Interior: (note: some differences exist between cars where customers specified different trim). All LHD. Racing seats and seatbelts with lightweight door panels and interior. Centre console removed. No sound insulation fitted. Weight: 2472lb (1121kg)

924 Carrera GTS Club Sport interior.

Club Sport option: Underbody protection removed. Internal aluminium roll bar fitted. Weight: 2336lb (1060kg)

924S (differences to 924 model)
Capacity: 2479cc water cooled four-cylinder. Wheels: 'telephone dial' alloy 6Jx15 (optional 6Jx16). Tyres: 195/65 VR15 (optional:205/55 VR16). Power steering: standard on US cars 1986 and European Automatic model, all models 1988. Some models have catalytic converters fitted. 1988 models have engine bhp increased from 150bhp to 160bhp.

924S engine bay.

Specials

A number of interesting specials were produced by the factory. There were also various companies offering conversions, including a rare Lainwather & Blazek 924 convertible conversion, one of just half a dozen cars known to be converted in the UK, of which there are only two Turbos.

Lainwather & Blazek 924 convertible conversion.

There were two TUV approved 'kits' to convert a 924 into a cabrio – one from Beiber, and one by Lainwather & Blazek, as used by 'Porkies Conversion' of Crediton on the car shown here.

Lainwather & Blazek 924 convertible from the rear.

Chassis numbers

From 1977 to 1979, 924 chassis numbers comprised ten digits, as follows:

Type	Model year	Version	Serial no
924	7	1	00001–on

Versions: 1=Europe; 2=USA; 3=Japan. In 1979, the 924 Turbo was given version number 4=Europe + rest of world (RoW); 5=USA + Japan.

From 1980, chassis were given a 17 digit number, an example of which, along with the code's meaning, is shown here:

WP0 ZZZ 92ZAN450001

W	West Germany
P	Porsche Automobil Holding SE
0	Sports car
Z	Domestic & RoW
Z	Not used
Z	Not used
92	Vehicle type designation (first two numbers)
Z	Not used
A	Year of manufacture (A=1980; B=1981; C=1982 etc)
N	Assembly plant (N=Neckarsulm)
4	Vehicle type designation (third number)
5	Engine body type (5=2.0-litre coupé USA spec)
0001	Chassis number

Vehicle designation codes:

Model	Code
924	924
924 Turbo	931
924 Carrera GT	937 (engine code = 0) Chassis nos. 0001-0006 = Weissach prototypes; chassis nos. 0051-0450 = Neckarsulm production models.
924 Carrera GTS	937 (engine code = 1) Chassis nos. 0001-0059
924S	924

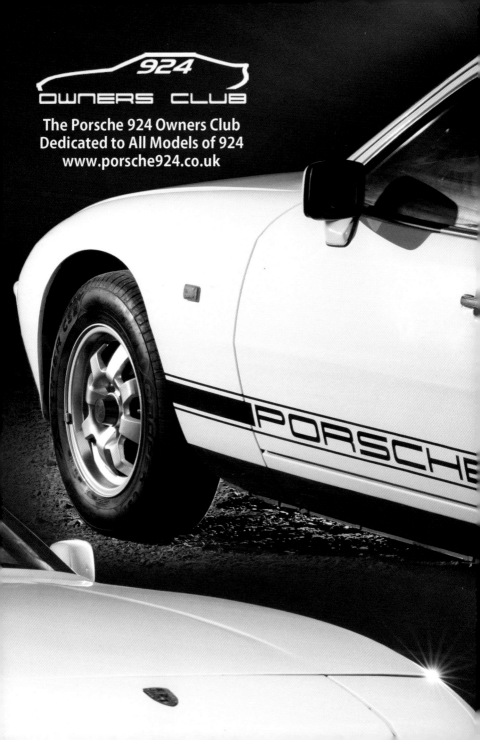

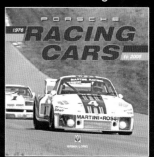

The Essential Buyer's Guide™ series ...

| 978-1-845840-22-8 | 978-1-845840-26-6 | 978-1-845840-29-7 | 978-1-845840-77-8 | 978-1-845840-99-0 | 978-1-845841-01-0 | 978-1-845841-07-2 | 978-1-845841-13-3 |

| 978-1-845841-19-5 | 978-1-845841-34-8 | 978-1-845841-35-5 | 978-1-845841-36-2 | 978-1-845841-38-6 | 978-1-845841-46-1 | 978-1-845841-47-8 | 978-1-845841-61-4 |

| 978-1-845841-63-8 | 978-1-845841-65-2 | 978-1-845841-88-1 | 978-1-845841-92-8 | 978-1-845842-00-0 | 978-1-845842-04-8 | 978-1-845842-05-5 | 978-1-845842-31-4 |

| 978-1-845842-70-3 | 978-1-845842-81-9 | 978-1-845842-83-3 | 978-1-845842-84-0 | 978-1-845842-87-1 | 978-1-845842-90-1 | 978-1-845843-03-8 | 978-1-845843-07-6 |

| 978-1-845843-09-0 | 978-1-845843-16-8 | 978-1-845843-29-8 | 978-1-845843-30-4 | 978-1-845843-34-2 | 978-1-845843-38-0 | 978-1-845843-39-7 |

£9.99 / $19.95 (prices subject to change, p&p extra).
For more details visit www.veloce.co.uk or email info@veloce.co.uk

... don't buy a vehicle until you've read one of these!

Index